HOW DOES IT WORK?
HOT AIR BALLOONS

by Nikole Brooks Bethea

pogo

Ideas for Parents and Teachers

Pogo Books let children practice reading informational text while introducing them to nonfiction features such as headings, labels, sidebars, maps, and diagrams, as well as a table of contents, glossary, and index.

Carefully leveled text with a strong photo match offers early fluent readers the support they need to succeed.

Before Reading

- "Walk" through the book and point out the various nonfiction features. Ask the student what purpose each feature serves.
- Look at the glossary together. Read and discuss the words.

Read the Book

- Have the child read the book independently.
- Invite him or her to list questions that arise from reading.

After Reading

- Discuss the child's questions. Talk about how he or she might find answers to those questions.
- Prompt the child to think more. Ask: What did you know about hot air balloons before you read this book? What more do you want to learn after reading it?

Pogo Books are published by Jump!
5357 Penn Avenue South
Minneapolis, MN 55419
www.jumplibrary.com

Library of Congress Cataloging-in-Publication Data

Names: Bethea, Nikole Brooks, author.
Title: Hot air balloons / by Nikole Brooks Bethea.
Description: Minneapolis, MN: Jump!, Inc., [2018]
Series: How does it work? | Audience: Ages 7-10.
Includes bibliographic references and index.
Identifiers: LCCN 2017031967 (print) | LCCN 2017030093 (ebook) | ISBN 9781624966972 (ebook)
ISBN 9781620319062 (hardcover: alk. paper)
ISBN 9781620319079 (pbk.)
Subjects: LCSH: Hot air balloons—Juvenile literature. Hot air balloons—History—Juvenile literature. Ballooning—Juvenile literature.
Classification: LCC TL638 (print)
LCC TL638 .B48 2017 (ebook) | DDC 629.133/22—dc23
LC record available at https://lccn.loc.gov/2017031967

Editors: Kirsten Chang & Jenna Trnka
Book Designer: Leah Sanders
Photo Researcher: Leah Sanders

Photo Credits: Brandon Bourdages/Shutterstock, cover; Samuel Acosta/Shutterstock, 1(left); tulpahn/Shutterstock, 1(right); Photomontage/Shutterstock, 3; shaunl/iStock, 4 (foreground); Evgeny Karandaev/Shutterstock, 4 (background); Mauro Rodrigues/Shutterstock, 5; Annette Shaff/Shutterstock, 6-7; southtownboy/iStock, 8-9; pio3/Shutterstock, 10; filo/iStock, 11; bildbroker.de/Alamy, 12-13; Leah Joy Kelton/Shutterstock, 14-15; Thitisan/Shutterstock, 16-17; Science Source/Getty, 18 (main); guteksk7/Shutterstock, 18 (tablet); Redorbital Photography/Alamy, 19; topseller/Shutterstock, 20-21; Patrick Foto/Shutterstock, 23.

Printed in the United States of America at Corporate Graphics in North Mankato, Minnesota.

TABLE OF CONTENTS

CHAPTER 1

FLOATING

Have you ever seen a hot air balloon? It rises in the sky. It floats among the clouds.

It has no motor.
It has no wings.
How does it fly?
Let's find out!

Think of a duck in water. Does it float or sink? It floats because it is less **dense** than the water. **Buoyancy** keeps it up.

Hot air balloons float because of buoyancy. This is an upward force. **Gravity** pulls things downward. Buoyancy acts against gravity.

buoyancy

gravity

hot air
molecules

cold air
molecules

What makes a balloon buoyant? Hot air.

Air is made of **molecules**. When air inside a balloon is heated, the air molecules expand. They move apart. There is more space between them. This makes the air less dense. The hot air inside weighs less than cold air outside the balloon. The hot air rises. It fills the fabric of the balloon. It lifts the whole thing up!

THINK ABOUT IT!

Imagine being inside a house on a hot summer day. Is it warmer or cooler in the basement? What does this prove about heat rising?

CHAPTER 2

· ·

PILOTING

Burners heat the air inside a balloon. They burn **propane** gas. This is the same gas used in barbeque grills.

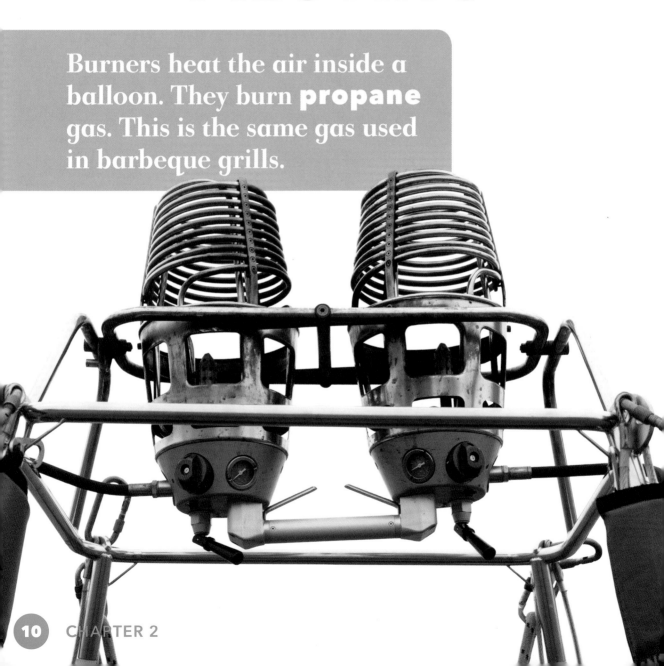

The burner is placed under the **envelope**. That is the fabric balloon that holds the air. It is usually made of nylon. Nylon works well because it has a high melting temperature.

envelope

The **pilot** and passengers stand in the basket. It hangs beneath the balloon. The basket is usually made of **wicker**. This is a light, flexible wood.

TAKE A LOOK!

What are the parts of a hot air balloon?

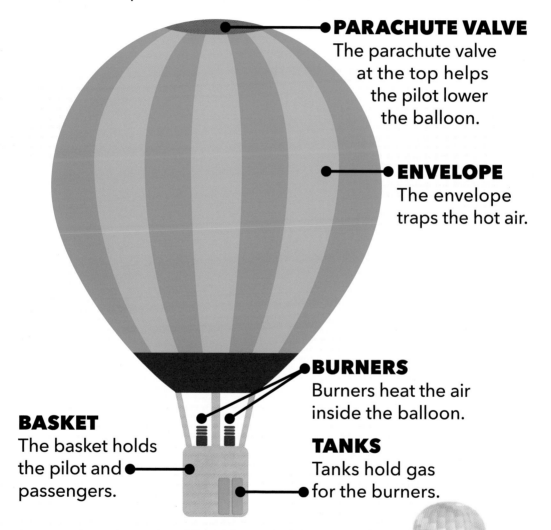

PARACHUTE VALVE
The parachute valve at the top helps the pilot lower the balloon.

ENVELOPE
The envelope traps the hot air.

BURNERS
Burners heat the air inside the balloon.

BASKET
The basket holds the pilot and passengers.

TANKS
Tanks hold gas for the burners.

To rise, the pilot opens the gas **valve**. This sends propane to the burner. More gas flow creates bigger flames. The air inside the balloon gets hotter. The balloon rises.

To sink, the pilot pulls a cord. It opens a valve at the top of the balloon. Hot air escapes. The temperature inside the balloon drops. The balloon sinks.

How does a balloon move from one place to another? The pilot depends on wind **currents**. Wind blows in different directions at different heights. The pilot moves up or down to catch a wind current. The balloon rides with the wind.

CHAPTER 3

BALLOONING

Hot air ballooning is the oldest form of flying. The first hot air balloon launched in France more than 200 years ago. Its passengers were a duck, a sheep, and a rooster!

Today's balloons are more advanced. In 2015, a **solar** balloon launched in the United Kingdom. One side of the balloon was black. It faced the sun to collect heat. The pilot used turning vents to keep the black side facing the sun. The other side was silver. It trapped the heat.

Balloon races are popular around the world. But they aren't races across a finish line. These races judge how close the pilot gets to a target. One task may be dropping a marker on a target on the ground. Another may be removing a ring from the top of a pole.

Hot air balloons are amazing flying machines. Would you like to ride in one?

ACTIVITIES & TOOLS

HOT AIR BALLOON ACTIVITY

Demonstrate how heat inflates and cold deflates a balloon in this activity.

What You Need:
- two pans or deep dishes
- hot and cold tap water
- empty 2-liter bottle
- deflated balloon
- ice

❶ Fill one pan or dish with hot tap water (not boiling).

❷ Fill the other pan or dish with cold tap water and ice.

❸ Remove the cap from the bottle.

❹ Blow the balloon up to stretch it. Deflate it.

❺ Stretch the opening of the balloon over the mouth of the bottle.

❻ Place the bottle in the hot water. You may need to hold it down. Wait a few minutes until the balloon begins to inflate. Why do you think this happens?

❼ Place the bottle and balloon in the ice water. Does the balloon deflate? Why?

GLOSSARY

buoyancy: The ability of an object to float.

currents: Continuous movements of air.

dense: Having parts that are compacted or crowded together; having a high mass per unit volume.

envelope: The fabric part of a hot air balloon that traps the air.

gravity: The attraction of the earth for bodies at or near its surface.

molecules: The smallest particles of a substance that have all the properties of the substance and are formed from one or more atoms that are bonded together.

pilot: Someone who operates the controls of an aircraft.

propane: A flammable gas used for cooking or heating.

solar: Operated by the sun's light or heat.

valve: A device that controls the flow of liquid or gas through a pipe.

wicker: Thin, dry branches or reeds that are woven together.

INDEX

TO LEARN MORE

Learning more is as easy as 1, 2, 3.

1) Go to www.factsurfer.com

2) Enter "hotairballoons" into the search box.

3) Click the "Surf" button to see a list of websites.

With factsurfer, finding more information is just a click away.